Bitcoin For E
Ediuon

An Introduction To Buying, Selling And Investing In Bitcoin In The UK

By Charles Stephens

Table of Contents

Introduction

Bitcoin is a technological revolution that has taken the financial world by storm! Opening 2017 at a value of $985, Bitcoin rose to a high of over $19,600 by the 19th December of the same year! These kind of exponential returns inevitably attracted widespread media attention, and while Bitcoin has dropped off since the highs of December 2017, the technology has shown that it is here to stay.

While the technology surrounding the Bitcoin and the blockchain is incredibly exciting and, in my opinion, has the potential to change the world, it can seem complex and intimidating to newcomers. This creates a barrier to entry for a number of potential users who would otherwise love to get involved in the technology. I have been invested in Bitcoin since 2014, and in the past year have become even more heavily involved in the Cryptocurrency space by getting involved at the ground floor in a number of Ethereum ICO Start Up Ventures. My aim for this book is to help you master the basics of buying and transacting with Bitcoin, particularly in reference to its usage in the UK. Most resources surrounding the technology tend to be US focused, so I'm hoping to help more people in the UK take their first step into the Cryptocurrency space by providing a resource tailor made for the UK Bitcoin market.

While some of the concepts discussed in this book are a little complicated, and slightly techy, I have tried to use analogies and examples to explain them in layman's terms to try and ease you into the concepts. Once you are comfortable with the examples presented in this book, I highly recommend diving deeper into your research and really immersing yourself into the technology! Hopefully by the end of this book you will agree that Bitcoin is here to stay and could have a huge impact on the world we live in!

Take heart in knowing that we are still very early in Bitcoin's journey! Many here the record prices and assume they are too late to 'join the party', but this isn't the case. Less than 2% of all American's own any amount of Bitcoin, and while accurate figures are not available for the UK, all estimates place the figure at lower adoption than in the US.

So knowing that you still have the opportunity to become an 'early adopter' of the most exciting technological phenomenon of the 21st Century, without further ado I will say thank you for purchasing this book and wish you all the best in your future Bitcoin journey!

What is Bitcoin?

The financial crisis of 2008 caused a lot of people to lose trust in banks as trusted third parties. This led to questions over whether banks were the best guardians of the global financial system. Bad investment decisions made by the major banks had proven catastrophic, the consequences of which were felt worldwide.

A new technology Bitcoin — also proposed in 2008 — presented something of an alternative.

According to its whitepaper, written by the anonymous Satoshi Nakamoto, Bitcoin was a "peer-to-peer electronic cash system." It would allow for online payments from one party to another without going through a financial institution."

In other words, Bitcoin technology made digital transactions possible without a "trusted intermediary." The technology allowed this to happen on a global scale, with cryptography carrying out the role that institutions such as commercial banks, financial regulators, and central banks had traditionally filled: verifying the legitimacy of transactions and safeguarding the integrity of the underlying asset.

Bitcoin is a decentralized, public ledger. There is no trusted third party controlling the ledger. Anyone who owns bitcoin can participate in the network, send and receive bitcoin, and even hold a copy of this ledger if they want to. In that sense, the ledger is "trustless" and transparent. In the wake of the 2008 financial crisis, this "trustless" ledger was Bitcoins biggest selling point.

The Bitcoin ledger tracks a single asset: bitcoin (Note: For the purposes of this book, "Bitcoin" capitalized refers to the Bitcoin ledger, or protocol, while "bitcoin" in lowercase refers to the currency or a unit of account on the Bitcoin ledger).

The ledger has rules encoded into it, the most famous of which states that there will only ever be 21M bitcoin produced. Because of this artificial cap on the number of bitcoins in circulation, which will eventually be reached, bitcoin is inherently resistant to inflation – in fact it is the world's first "deflationary currency". That means that more bitcoin can't be printed at a whim and reduce the overall value of the currency.

All participants must agree to the ledger's rules in order to use it. Any change from the agreed rules will result in a "Hard Fork" and an entirely new cryptocurrency being developed (i.e. Litecoin or Bitcoin Cash).

Bitcoin is politically decentralized, meaning no single entity runs bitcoin — but centralized from a data standpoint, in that all participants (nodes) agree on the state of the ledger and its rules.

A bitcoin or a transaction can't be edited, erased, copied, or forged – every other user on the network would be able to see when the amendment was made and who did it and the change would not be verified onto the ledger.

And that's my crash course in Bitcoin complete. Keep in mind that it is only a very basic overview, and far from comprehensive. However, I hope it serves as a good introduction to the technology. I highly recommend further research online after completing this book – for those interested, topics such as the first Bitcoin transaction (Google "bitcoin pizza") or the upcoming Lightning payment network would be good places to start.

A Brief History Of Bitcoin – Highlights (and Lowlights) Of The First 10 Years

2008 – The Legend of Satoshi Nakamoto

On the 31st October 2008, someone working under the alias of Satoshi Nakamoto published the Bitcoin whitepaper - "Bitcoin: A Peer-to-Peer Electronic Cash System"[1], which outlines the concept of the bitcoin. Most notably this paper addresses the problem of double spending, so as to avoid the currency being copied and spent twice. This was an essential foundation brick, which separated Bitcoin from previous digital currencies that had all suffered from this issue.

In August 20018, shortly before the whitepaper was published, Bitcoin.org was born. The whois entry for the site shows the domain was registered in Panama, but the sire used to register the domain allows its users to buy and register domain names anonymously.

If we think back to August 2008, it was just weeks before the collapse of Lehman Brothers and the financial meltdown - a time when banks were notorious for underhand dealings and behaving as they pleased. Bitcoin was created as a decentralised alternative for traditional banking, controlled and monitored by market forces rather than banks and governments.

2009 – Bitcoin is released to the public

In early 2009, Bitcoin software is made available to the public for the first time. The first ever block is mined – which has since become affectionately known as the Genesis Block. Mining is the process by which new Bitcoins can be created. The transactions are recorded and verified on the Bitcoin blockchain. The first ever Bitcoin transaction occurred between Satoshi and Hal Finney, a fellow Bitcoin developer and cryptographic supporter.

By the end of 2009, the first bitcoin exchange rate is established and published. Bitcoin receives a value like a traditional currency. At this point $1 = 1309 Bitcoin (1 Bitcoin = 0.00077 USD)

2010 – The Infamous Pizza Transaction

As global economies continued to recover from the financial crash, the first ever real world Bitcoin transaction occurred when a Florida programmer paid 10,000 bitcoins for delivery of two pizzas worth around $25. This is considered one of the most significant moments in Bitcoin history, as it represented the first real world usage of the young currency.

Later that year bitcoin was hacked for the first time, drawing attention to one its principal weaknesses; security. Bitcoin's value had grown and was trading at around $1 prior to the hack, which then sent the value through the floor. Further bad press this same year, which suggested it could be used to fund terrorist groups through dark net website The Silk Road further hurt the coins popularity.

2011 – Achieving Parity With The Dollar

Bitcoin reached parity with the dollar for the first time in 2011. By June of the same year Bitcoins value had spiked to $31, which meant the coins total market cap had reached $206 million. 25% of the finite total of 21 million bitcoins had now been mined. The first 'altcoins' such as Litecoin were now appearing as adoption in the space increases.

2013 – Bitcoin Struggles - Security Issues And Price Crashes

June of 2013 saw a major theft of bitcoin take place from a digital wallet – once again leading to questions surrounding the cryptocurrencies security. In the same year, another major security breech saw the value of bitcoin tumble from $17.50 to just $0.01. 2013 also saw the US Financial Crimes Enforcement Network issue the first bitcoin regulation. This would be the start of an ongoing debate as to how best regulate the virtual currency. During this year, Bitcoin's market cap reached $1 billion for the first time.

2014 – Mt.Gox disappears along with 850,000 bitcoins

This year was characterised by growing understanding and desire to regulate bitcoin. Not surprising after the world's largest bitcoin exchange Mt.Gox suddenly went offline and 850,000 bitcoins were never seen again. Often referred to as Bitcoins darket day, there is still no clear answer to what happened to those Bitcoins, valued at the time at $450 million, but at today's value those coins would be worth over $3 billion.

2016 – Bitcoin boomed

During 2016, Bitcoin saw an annual gain of 54% - outperforming all fiat currencies. This was the year that bitcoin really started establishing itself and provided holders of the currency various ways to generate a return or indeed use the currency. Bitcoin began to be seen as a safe haven from traditional assets in a turbulent year of Brexit, Donald Trump winning the US Presidency, the continued rise of ISIS and the refugee crisis in Europe.

2017 – Legitimacy and Hitting The Mainstream

During 2017, the value of bitcoin jumped from $985 to over $19,661 and its popularity has soared exponentially. The currency went mainstream as it became listed on two Wall Street Futures exchanges - CBOE and CME. The listing of Bitcoin Future contracts on these exchanges boosted the legitimacy of bitcoin and made it more widely available. Despite the futures contracts providing ability to short bitcoin, the value of the cryptocurrency hits an all-time high in December 2017.

Bitcoin In Action

The story of Amanda and Bill

To understand better how this peer-to-peer electronic cash system (bitcoin) allows for online payments to move from one party (individual) to another without going through a financial institution, let's use a simple example.

Here's a scenario: Amanda hands Bill a physical $5 arcade token. Bill now has one token, and Amanda has zero. The transaction is complete. Amanda and Bill do not need an intermediary to verify the transaction. Amanda can't give her friend Christopher the same token, because she no longer has the token to give — she already gave it to Bill.

But what if that same transaction took place digitally? Amanda sends Bill a digital arcade token — via email or WhatsApp, for example. Bill should now have the digital token, and Amanda should not.

But not so fast… What if Amanda made a copy or "forgery" of the digital arcade token? What if Amanda put a copy the same digital token online that anybody could now download? After all, a digital token is just a string of ones and zeros.

If Amanda and Bill "own" the same string of ones and zeros, who is the true owner of the digital token? If digital assets can be reproduced so easily, what stops Amanda from trying to "spend" the same digital asset twice by also sending it to Christopher?

How can Amanda and Bill establish unique ownership over the digital token?

One answer: use a database — a ledger. This ledger will track a single asset: in this case, digital arcade tokens. When Amanda gives Bill the digital token, the ledger records the transaction. Bill now has the token, and Amanda does not.

A trusted third party, an intermediary — let's call him Dan — will hold the ledger and make sure that it's kept up-to-date. Amanda can't hold the ledger because she might erase the transaction and claim that she still owns the digital token, even though in reality she already gave it to Bill. It also can't be Bill, because he could alter the transaction and lie to say that Amanda gave him two tokens, doubling his arcade time.

To ensure the ledgers integrity, Dan — who is not involved in the transaction at all, will have to control the ledger. In this case, Dan is trusted.

This is the role filled by traditional banking, and the situation tends to work fine… until it's doesn't.

What if Dan decides to charge a fee for his services of updating the ledger that neither Amanda or Bill want to pay? Or, what if Amanda offers Dan a bribe to erase her transaction from the ledger? Maybe Dan will decide that actually he wants the digital token for himself, so adds a false transaction to the ledger in order to embezzle it, saying that Bill gave him the token?

In other words — what happens when Amanda and Bill cannot trust the trusted third party?

Let's go back to the first physical transaction between Amanda and Bill. Is there a way to make digital transactions look more like that?

Here's a thought: Amanda and Bill could distribute the ledger to all their trusted friends, not just Dan, and decentralize trust. Because the ledger is digital, all copies of the ledger could sync together. If a simple majority of participants agree that the transaction is valid (e.g. confirm that Amanda actually owns the token she is trying to send), it gets added to the ledger.

When lots of people have a copy of the same ledger, it becomes much more difficult to cheat. If Amanda or Bill wanted to falsify a transaction, they would have to bribe or trick the majority of participants, which is much more difficult than compromising a single participant.

Amanda now can't claim that she never sent a digital token to Bill — her version of the ledger would not agree with everyone else's. Similarly, Bill couldn't claim that Amanda gave him two tokens — his ledger would now be out of sync. And even if Amanda bribes Dan to change his copy of the ledger, Dan now only holds a single copy of the ledger; the majority opinion would still show the digital token was sent and is now in Bill's possession.

In short, this distributed ledger works because everyone is now holding a copy of the same digital ledger. The more trusted people that hold the ledger, the stronger it becomes.

Such a ledger allows Amanda to send a digital token to Bill without having to go through Dan. In a sense she is transforming her digital transaction into something that looks more like a physical one in the real world, where ownership and scarcity of an asset is tangible, measurable and obvious.

Is Bitcoin really secure?

You may have noticed a key difference between the example in the previous chapter and Bitcoin. Specifically, Amanda's and Bill's ledger only allows their "trusted friends" to participate. In contrast, Bitcoin is entirely public, meaning that anyone can participate.

How can we get all these untrusted "nodes" (participants keeping the ledger up to date) to agree on the state of the ledger? How can we avoid bad actors corrupting the ledger?

Let's think about this for a moment. A public ledger allows for many more participants, and the more participants, the stronger the ledger automatically becomes. Right?

As you may have guessed, in reality it's not that simple.

Because Bitcoin expands beyond only using trusted participants and gives anyone access, it runs a higher risk of bad actors and false transactions.

Sure, we also ran a risk of bad actors in our previous example using only Amanda's and Bill's trusted friends – for example, Dan might turn untrustworthy. However, Bitcoin is free and open to anyone, trusted or not, like a shared Google document that anyone can read and write to.

So the key question here is:

How can we get all these untrusted "nodes" to agree on the state of the ledger? How can we avoid bad actors corrupting the ledger?

Here, Bitcoin offers a solution: reward the good actors and scare off the bad ones, a classic carrot and stick act.

In simple terms, certain Bitcoin participants are incentivized to do the hard yards and maintain the network. These participants — referred to as "miners" — bundle pending transactions into a "block". Once verified by a miner, this newest block is added on to the "chain" of prior blocks (hence why the term "blockchain" is used to describe Bitcoin's unique database structure). Mincers devote immense computational power to the network in the process. Miners are incentivized to carry out this work by a "Block Reward". Currently the Block Reward is set at 25 bitcoins, although this would drop to 12.5 bitcoins at some point in 2020 at the time of the next Bitcoin Halvening.

When miners devote computational power, they also use a tremendous amount of electricity. So much electricity, in fact, that a recent estimate put the Bitcoin blockchains total daily energy consumption at greater than Ecuador's, a country of 17M people.

This system is designed to disincentivise hackers and bad actors because "hacking" Bitcoin to get access to other peoples coins would cost a tremendous amount of computing power, electricity, and money. Further, if the Bitcoin community found out about the hack (which is likely due to the decentralized ledger), it would likely cause the price of bitcoin to drop sharply.

Thus such an attack becomes economically self-defeating.

In technical terms, this mining process creates Bitcoin's consensus mechanism, called "Proof of Work."

This clever game-theoretic model creates a ledger that everyone trusts, but nobody controls.

Where to buy Bitcoin

Now that we have covered the basics of Bitcoin, we will now cover a few methods of how you can purchase your very own Bitcoin today!

To purchase Bitcoin you will need to sign up to a website such as coinbase.com or use an "Exchange" where you can buy and sell Bitcoin to and from other users. While the market value generally prevents too much variation between selling prices (these quickly get eaten up by arbitrage trading), the fees between Exchanges do vary wildly. I will set out the fees involved in all of my recommended exchanges below.

Note that many other exchanges are available, but I have found the following to be the best options – dependent on the scenario.

The Easiest way to Purchase Bitcoin in the UK

Coinbase.com

The easiest and quickest way to buy bitcoin in the UK is through Coinbase with a debit or credit card. Based out of San Francisco, Coinbase allow users to buy with USD, Euros and, most importantly, GBP. Coinbase is the currently the largest cryptocurrency exchange in operation, with reportedly over 15 million registered users. They also offer their services across 32 countries.

Coinbase's sign up process is fairly straight forward, although due to KYC (Know Your Customer) rules in the UK you will be required to verify your identity. This will come in the form of your passport or driving licence, so be sure to sign up with the exact name you have on the documentation you will be using to verify your identity. For further information on

Coinbase's identity verification process see their website: https://support.coinbase.com/customer/en/portal/articles/1220621-identity-verification

Once your identity is verified, you will be free to start buying Bitcoin! Coinbase will display their current "instant buy" price on their homepage (along with their prices for other cryptocurrencies such as Ethereum, Litecoin and Bitcoin Cash). Be sure you have Bitcoin selected when you make your purchase!

There are two payment types you can choose when purchasing from Coinbase in the UK. The first option is to purchase via Credit/Debit Card. This is the fastest way to purchase bitcoin, as the transaction is completed instantly and the Bitcoin is immediately added to your account. The downside to this method is that a 3.99% transaction fee is charged by Coinbase to process your transaction. So if you were to purchase £1000 worth of Bitcoin via credit card, the transaction fee would be 39.99, making your total cost 1039.99.

The second payment option is to use a SEPA transfer. This option avoids the fees faced when paying by credit card, but also much slower. SEPA transfers can also only be sent in Euro's meaning that you are subject to your banks exchange rate and a possible fee for currency exchange. We will cover how to minimise exchange rate fees later in the book. A SEPA can also take 2-3 days to be approved by your bank account, and a further 2-5 days to clear into your Coinbase account. You could be waiting a week to get access to your funds, which in the world of cryptocurrency can feel like a lifetime!

Once you have decided your payment method and made your purchase, your Bitcoin will automatically be deposited into your Coinbase Bitcoin Wallet. This currency is now free for you to use, send and spend however you please!

Option 2 – Using GDAX.com

GDAX.com is a Bitcoin Exchange owned by Coinbase. While the exchange lacks the intuitive UI and speed of use that Coinbase has, it does have the advantage of having much lower (zero) fees and a lower buy price than Coinbase (Coinbase's "Instant Buy" price has a premium added on to the GDAX spot price.

You will have to sign up again to GDAX, and verify your identity again (you need a verified Coinbase account to sign up to GDAX). Once verified, you can add a bank account to GDAX and set up a SEPA transfer to your account. Again SEPA transfers can only be carried out in Euros, and GDAX has no GBP deposit option.

Once you have funds in your account, you can either purchase at GDAX's spot price (and pay a 0.30% transaction fee) or you can avoid fees altogether by placing what's known as a 'Maker' order.

In order to be considered a 'Maker', you need to enter the amount of Bitcoin you want to purchase and the price you want to purchase at . You also want to make sure you check the box that says "Post Only" as well as set the "Time In Force Policy" to "Good Till Cancelled".

The fastest way to getting your buy order filled is by accurately filling out the 'Maker' price to reflect the current market price. GDAX shows you all the current buy orders being filled inside the "Order Book" section of its dashboard. Look at the buy orders being filled and put your 'Maker' price equal to the last buy order.

Once your order is placed you will be added to the "Order Book", which is filled with all of the Limit Orders placed on GDAX. You will need other Bitcoin users to be willing to sell at the price you have entered. If nobody is willing to sell at the price you have entered, then your order will never be filled. The order book works from the highest price down (so a 10,000 GBP Limit Order will be filled before an £5,000 GBP Limit Order), and orders of the same value are filled oldest to newest. Once enough sales have been entered and your order has been filled, Coinbase will add your Bitcoin to your GDAX bitcoin wallet.

Choosing whether to use Coinbase or GDAX comes down to how sensitive you are to time and to fees. Coinbase's "instant buy" is very convenient and allows you to purchase Bitcoin instantly, whereas using GDAX to avoid fees will save you a few percent in transaction fees but will take an unspecified amount of time to fill your order. Whether fees or time are more important to you is a decision you will have to make for yourself.

Option 3 – Using Revolut/GDAX.com

The Revolut to GDAX method is one of the most popular methods used in the UK Bitcoin community when purchasing new bitcoin. This method allows you to purchase your bitcoin at the best possible price, by eliminating the transaction fees and SEPA fees discussed in options 1 and 2. The reason Revolut can offer free SEPA transfers to its customers is that the free account Revolut offer includes both a GBP and a EUR account for all of their British customers. By transferring funds from your GBP Revolut account to your EUR Revolut account you will receive one of the best exchange rates on the market, and you can then SEPA the funds directly into your Coinbase account. Please note that this route is the slowest of all of the options listed, and does not work on weekends. SEPA transfers only get pushed through during normal banking hours – i.e. Monday AM to

Friday PM. For weekend purchases, we recommend using either Coinbase or Localbitcoins (listed below).

Summary of this process:

1. Sign up for both Coinbase and Revolut
2. Transfer GBP funds into your Revolut GBP account
3. Activate your EUR wallet
4. Convert your GBP funds into EUR in Revolut (FREE)
5. Send EUR to Coinbase (FREE)
6. Transfer EUR from Coinbase to GDAX (FREE)
7. Buy bitcoin on the BTC/EUR market

How to Purchase Bitcoin's Anonymously – Localbitcoins.com

All exchanges must have a verification process for UK customers due to the Know Your Customer regulations that affect financial institutions. However, some are averse to sharing their identity in order to buy Bitcoin. For these people, the best option to purchase Bitcoin is to use services such as localbitcoins.com. Services such as Local Bitcoin generally charge a premium over online exchanges due to the nature of the transactions and the ability of each individual seller to set their own price.

For anyone looking to buy Bitcoins anonymously then the easiest way would be to buy Bitcoins in cash and in person. Local Bitcoins allows you to find someone who is willing to sell Bitcoins for cash near to your physical location. You can use an alias email address to sign up to Local Bitcoins and the verification id process they have is optional. When you use cash it's easy to remain untraceable as there is no documentation for the transaction. It is important to keep in mind that most sellers on Local Bitcoins don't like to do business with anonymous buyers, with some charging an additional premium for cash transactions over PayPal transactions.

Most Local Bitcoins sellers will allow PayPal purchases ranging between 10 USD to 1500 USD. The big downside is that they require you to have community reputation (previous purchase history). Sellers do this in-order to minimize the risk that bad-actors reverse the PayPal transaction while keeping the bitcoins. Note that using PayPal rather than cash will create a digital trail, and the transaction will lose its Anonymity.

Other Exchanges to consider

The below are highly trustworthy and popular exchanges. The reason I have recommended Coinbase/GDAX above the below exchanges is due to ease of use and the fact that none of the below accept GBP as a deposit option. All of the below will require a SEPA transfer in Euros (again we recommend using a Revolut account to purchase from any of these European exchanges in order to avoid fees).

Bitstamp.net

Gemini.com

Kraken.com

How To Sell Bitcoin In The UK

In general you are able to sell Bitcoin back to the majority of sites from which you are able to buy them. As with buying Bitcoin, there is generally a trade-off between transaction fees and transaction fees.

Selling On GDAX.com

My recommended route to sell Bitcoin in the UK is to essentially reverse the Revolut/GDAX method discussed in the previous chapter. When selling on GDAX.com, there are two types of sellers – 'Makers' and 'Takers'. For orders placed or sold at current market value you are considered a 'Taker', and will be charged a transaction fee of 0.30% for your sale. However, if you place a sell order at above market value (add it to the order book) and it is filled by a buyer in the 'Taker' role, you will not be charged any transaction fee for your sale.

Example:

Current Market Value = 1,000 EUR

Amanda places sell order at 1,000 EUR, filled immediately (fees paid = 0.30% - 3.00 EUR)

Amanda places sell order at 1,005 EUR, filled by Bill 2 hours later (fees paid = 0)

Of course the danger is that the market value may take time to rise to your 'Maker' sale value, which is why some are willing to pay the 0.30% 'Taker' fee to ensure an immediate sale. If you plan to use the Revolut method, you will need to make your sale on the BTC/EUR market as you cannot convert between currencies within Coinbase.

Once you have completed your sale, your Euro funds will be added to your EUR wallet on GDAX. From here you will need to transfer the EUR funds back into your Coinbase account in order to SEPA into your Revolut EUR account. Next, we want to transfer the EUR funds into our GBP Revolut account – taking advantage of Revolut's preferential exchange rate. Once you have the funds in your GBP Revolut wallet, you are free to either spend them from your Revolut account or to transfer the funds to your existing bank account. This entire process will cost a total of £0.15.

Summary of this process:

1. Log In to GDAX and click on 'Withdraw Funds' while in the EUR/BTC market
2. Transfer EUR funds to your Coinbase Account (FREE)
3. Go to Coinbase > Accounts > Euro Wallet > Withdraw
4. Log In to Revolut and go into your EUR wallet > Top Up > Bank Transfer > EUR
5. Note down your IBAN and BIC numbers for your EUR Revolut account, and enter them into Coinbase. Also include the total amount you wish to withdraw (in Euros).
6. Withdraw funds into Revolut (15p charge)
7. Once funds are showing in your Revolut EUR account, exchange from EUR to GBP (FREE)
8. Now go to your GBP wallet > send funds. Add yourself as a beneficiary.
9. Send the funds to your existing bank account! (free)

Of course, there is the option to withdraw the funds directly from Coinbase to your UK bank account. However, you'll lose a percentage of your funds (typically more than 1%) in your banks foreign exchange rate conversion (from EUR to GBP) when your bank processes the transfer. It is also worth noting some UK banks do not accept deposits from Bitcoin Exchanges such as Coinbase, so it is worth checking with your bank if they will accept the deposit before sending – particularly for large transactions.

Please note – Please do not sell on the BTC/GBP market on GDAX if you are looking to cash out. Coinbase do not currently offer a GBP wallet, so funds will be stuck on GDAX. This is the main reason the Revolut option is so popular amongst UK bitcoiners.

Selling On Localbitcoins.com

As before for those worried about anonymity, or for those unable to sell in Euros and only wanting to transact in GBP, localbitcoins.com would be a good option. Local bitcoins also has the benefit of allowing you access to your funds same day (usually funds are available in less than an hour), as transactions are completed in GBP and you are able to transfer directly to your UK bank account from the localbitcoins.com website.

In exchange for this convenience, you'll usually get offered a sale price which is below the going market rate (usually up to 5%, but at times this can be more). Of course, you are able to set up your own sell orders on local bitcoins (so you are actually able to sell at above market rate), however this would involve vetting your own buyers which can be difficult even for experienced traders and opens you up to scams and time wasters. This would also remove the 'instant' benefit of using local bitcoins, as you would need to wait for someone to fill your sell order. I recommend beginners stay away from this option, so pursue at your own risk.

Tax Implications Of Selling Bitcoin

Despite much confusion surrounding the subject, tax does apply to profit gains from cryptocurrencies in the UK, however to many it doesn't seem to be strictly enforced due to a current lack of regulation. Historically, it appears that tax on cryptocurrencies has, for the most part, been ignored by many until contacted/chased by HMRC (Her Majesty's Revenue and Customs). However this is not advisable, as interest and fines may be applied to the tax owed if HMRC have to chase you up for late payment. I highly advise that you pay any tax owed on cryptocurrency transactions on time and in full per the below parameters.

There are two different types of tax that should concern general investors, only one of which applies to your cryptocurrency profits -These are Income Tax and Capital Gains. Each of these have annual allowances that apply to each individual, allowing a set amount of income or capital gains before paying tax. The personal Income tax allowance for the 2018 tax year was £11,500 (increasing to £11,850 for the 2019 tax year), and the Capital gains allowance (or Annual Exempt Amount) for the 2018 tax year was £11,300 (increasing to £11,700 for the 2019 tax year)[2].

Income tax will generally apply to mining activities, so assuming we are only investing in Bitcoin through exchanges such as Coinbase the only tax rate we need to consider the Capital Gains Tax. For the 2018 Tax year our Capital Gains allowance was £11,300, meaning we could earn up to £11,300 in **profit** from our Bitcoin investments before we had to pay any tax to HMRC (assuming we cashed out no other investments to use up our allowance).

Consider the two examples below:

Scenario 1 (No taxed owed):

- Initial investment £1k into BTC
- Over time, the investment increases in value and is now worth £12.3k
- We sell our entire portfolio, and deposit £12.3k into our bank account
- Our total profit for the investment is £11.3k (£12.3k sale value - £1k initial investment)
- This means we have used our entire £11,300 Capital Gains allowance for the year, but we have NOT exceeded it.
- Total Tax Owed = £0 (but any further sales of BTC will be taxed at our standard Capital Gains tax rate)

Scenario 2 (Exceeding the Capital Gains Allowance):

- Initial investment £1k into BTC
- Over time, the investment increases in value and is now worth £15k
- We decided to cash out half of our initial investment – now worth £7.5k.
- Our profit at this stage is £7k (£7.5k sale value – half our initial £1k investment)
- Later in the same tax year, our remaining BTC is now worth £9k and we decide to cash the remainder of our investment.
- Our profit for this second transaction is £8.5k (£9k sale value – half our initial investment)
- Our total profit for the tax year is now £15.5k (£7k + £8.5k)

- Our Capital Gains Allowance for the tax year is £11.3k, meaning that we owe tax on **3.2k** of our profits (£15.5k - £11.3k)
- Assuming basic Capital Gains Rate of 20%, our total tax bill for the tax year would be **£640** (£3.2k x 20%)

Capital Gains Tax is based on how much the value of an asset changed. If you've made more than £11,300 in profits, you'll need to fill out a self-assessment tax return for that tax year. You can register for one online on the governments website: https://www.gov.uk/self-assessment-tax-returns/sending-return (click whichever applies to you under point 3 - self-employed, not self-employed etc.).

While this is the most simple option, and should serve the majority of investors, there are a few options available. If you make sufficient bitcoin profits and want to minimise your taxes, then it may make sense to operate via a limited company, pay yourself an income, pay the capital gains tax with the company, and then take the rest as a dividend (tax free). You won't be able to set this up retroactively though, you could only apply this to profits made after you have a limited company registered.

How Should I Store My Bitcoin

Now that you have successfully purchased your bitcoin, you now have to decide how you are going to store your Bitcoin. There are essentially three options when it comes to storing bitcoin – storing your bitcoin in an exchange wallet, moving it to a 'hot' wallet or moving it to a 'cold wallet'. There are pro's and con's for each of these methods, so it is down to the individual to decide which method is best for them.

Storing On An Exchange

As soon as you purchase your bitcoin, the exchange will transfer your funds to your personal wallet on the exchange website. These funds are now available for you to move or sell as you see fit. Storing your funds on an exchange wallet requires no action on your part and is the easiest method of storing your bitcoins. However while this is the most popular method of storage for newcomers to bitcoin, there are a few drawbacks that should be noted before committing yourself to this option.

Firstly, and most importantly, is that you do not own your own private keys for your bitcoin. Without getting too technical, the private key is what identifies the bitcoin you own as yours. With the private keys you are able to recover bitcoins from lost wallets, and claim any forked coins (i.e. Bitcoin Cash) for yourself. Without the private keys you are relying on the exchange to manage your bitcoin for you, and may miss out on forks if the exchange decides not to support them. While the exchange holds your private keys, they control your bitcoin.

Secondly, you are trusting the exchange to stay solvent and protect your bitcoin. In the short history of bitcoin, exchanges have not been the most stable entities. Infamously, Mt. Gox lost millions of dollars' worth of its users coins in 2014 following a series of security breaches. More recently exchange hacks have made the news during bitcoins exponential price increase at the back end of 2017. Should the exchange you trust with your coins go out of business or get hacked, you may up losing all of your coins with no private key to claim them back.

For the reasons above, I recommend all newcomers move their coins out of their exchange wallets. GDAX offer free transfers out of their exchange wallet, so users will save on the small transaction fee usually required to move Bitcoin. If customers insist on using an exchange wallet, I will generally suggest Coinbase as they are the largest and most professional exchange currently in operation. However, it is worth noting that Mt. Gox has ~70% of all bitcoin trading volume when they were hacked in 2014 (admittedly trading volume was much lower back then) so size doesn't necessarily mean that coins are safe.

So if we need to move our coins off of an exchange, where should we be sending them?

Hot Wallet Option

A 'hot' wallet is any wallet that is run connected to the internet. Typically these wallets will come in the form of a downloadable desktop program or a mobile app. Hot wallets are more convenient than cold wallets as they are always available, but I would not recommend hot wallets for large holdings. Due to their internet connection, they are vulnerable to malware and backdoors, with hackers increasingly targeting desktop wallets with the recent surge in price. Desktop wallets also run the risk of being exposed to malware already on a compute/laptop upon install, with keylogging a particular worry for this software.

However hot wallets do give you control of your own private keys, making them an upgrade on an exchange wallet and a perfectly acceptable option for storing small amounts of cryptocurrency.

Some popular hot wallet options:

- Breadwallet: Simple and beginner friendly mobile wallet. My personal recommendation for a hot wallet for a new investor.
- Electrum: Open source wallet. Available on both desktop and mobile, but more complicated than other wallet options.
- Exodus: This wallet has a great user interface and supports multiple cryptocurrencies. A good choice for beginners interested in investing in more than one crypto coin.

Cold Wallet Option

While hot wallets are connected to the internet, a 'cold' wallet is a wallet that is completely offline. This protects the wallet from being affected from malware, and also from hacking attempts. While there are multiple forms of cold storage (i.e. paper wallets), for beginners I always recommend using a hardware wallet.

A hardware wallet is a small, USB device which allows you to store multiple cryptocurrencies. They are completely secure as all of the information is stored internally on the device, which is run completely separate to the computer it is plugged into. This means you could plug a hardware wallet into a computer completely riddled with malware, and the malware would have no way of infecting or interacting with your hardware wallet and your coins would be completely safe! While hardware wallets are not quite as secure as true cold storage (i.e. paper wallets), they are **much** safer than the hot wallet alternative. They are also easy to use, as you simply plug the hardware wallet into your computer or laptops USB port.

The major drawback of a hardware wallet is the initial outlay required. The two major brands can typically be purchased for between £70 and £100. Although it is not mandatory, I typically recommend investors with more than £1000 invested in bitcoin make the investment and purchase a hardware wallet. The initial investment is more than covered by the peace of mind of knowing that your coins are safe.

Popular, well-recommended hardware wallet options include the:

- Ledger Nano S
- Trezor

Both of the above are reputable and will serve you well. At the current time of writing, the Ledger Nano S is slightly cheaper and offers support for more cryptocurrencies than the Trezor. However, unless you need the greater cryptocurrency support, the difference between the two is negligible. For the sake of transparency, I personally use the Ledger Nano S to protect my investments and have been very pleased with the devices performance to date.

Usage Note: When setting up your hardware wallet, I recommend that you do **not** record your 24 word mnemonic seed (which you use to restore the wallet) on a digital device. Instead, record this recovery seed offline on a piece of paper or card. Both devices supply cards to record the mnemonic seed on, so the best option is to use these.

The Future Of Bitcoin

2017 was certainly an eventful year for Bitcoin, with plenty of positives and negatives throughout the year. The main talking point for the majority of the year was the contentious and bitter hard fork attempt by Bitcoin Cash. While the fork did find some support and is still trading (at around 10% of Bitcoin's value at time of writing), ultimately BTC won the 'coin war' of 2017, despite a heavy FUD (Fear, Uncertainty, Doubt) war between the two sides online.

Almost as soon as the hard fork was resolved, public interest in Bitcoin hit unprecedented levels. This led to the price surge at the back end of 2017, which was Bitcoins market value peak at more than $19,400 in December 2017. The value has since fallen away in early 2018, but remains in a strong position.

While 2017 was the year that Bitcoin made huge advances in public awareness and public perception, 2018 promises to be the year of technological advances - with the highly anticipated Lightning Network Beta released onto the MainNet in March 2018, and the full release promised later this year.

Lightning Network

Imagine if your computer had to store every e-mail ever sent in order to be able to receive any new messages. In essence, that's how blockchains work. The Lightning Network will allow computers to separate blockchain transactions, meaning they only store the data they care about—their own money.

Lightning Network is a protocol for scaling and speeding up blockchains. It was designed primarily to help solve some of the technical limitations of the Bitcoin blockchain, but could theoretically be implemented on top of any blockchain.

Improving scalability was the first major motivator for developing the Lightning Network, as the distributed nature of Bitcoin greatly limits the transaction rate of the network. While Visa can process tens of thousands of transactions per second, Bitcoin's network is limited to less than 10 transactions per second. Another motivator for the Lightning Networks development is that the Bitcoin blockchain's "block confirmation time" is approximately 10 minutes. This means it takes at least 10 minutes for a bitcoin transaction to confirm. On top of this, transaction fees on the Bitcoin blockchain can run between 5 and 10 cents per transaction, making small 'micropayments' infeasible. Lightning Network, by contrast, can enable near-instant transactions, at a rate of thousands to millions of transactions per second, with fees of only a fraction of a cent (or potentially even free).

Lightning Network is based on a technology called payment channels. A two-party payment channel is created when two parties create a 2-out-of-2 multi signature transaction on the blockchain, with at least one party committing funds to the 2-of-2 ledger entry. Each person holds one private key, and transactions spending from the ledger entry can now be made only if both keys sign. The initial transaction to open a new channel will take 10 minutes (or whatever the normal block time is), but subsequently the participants are able to transact with each other instantly using the funds allocated in the channel. These instantaneous transactions are made by passing signed transactions back and forth, spending from the 2-of-2 ledger entry.

Each transaction would be valid if broadcast to the network and included in the blockchain by the network's miners, but in a payment channel, those signed transactions are not broadcast until the participants want the channel to stop operating (i.e. they close the channel or remove all funds from the channel). Signed but unbroadcast transactions are exchanged using direct, peer-to-peer communication, and held like redeemable receipts by the participants.

Let's go back to our earlier example using Amanda and Bill. Using the Lightning Network, Amanda and Bill create an initial transaction on the blockchain for a value of $20, where each party has $10 of the value.

This initial allocation can then be updated, such that Amanda then has $5 of the total $20 value, and Bill has $15 (Amanda has paid Bill $5), and so on. When the participants have concluded transacting with each other, the most recently exchanged transaction signature is broadcast to the network, finalising the movement of the funds in the channel—some to one party and (if any remain) some back to the other.

The Lightning Network takes the technology behind payment channels and creates a network of these channels, utilising "smart contracts" to ensure that the network can function in a decentralized capacity without counterparty risk. As an example, Amanda may open a channel with Bill, who in turn has a channel open with Christopher, who has one open with Dan. If Amanda wants to transact with Dan, she can send funds via Bill and Christopher, and Dan will ultimately receive them. But, because of the multi signature and smart contracts inherent in the design of Lightning, Amanda doesn't need to trust Bill and Christopher as intermediaries—the protocol uses cryptography to ensure that the funds will either reach Dan through Bill and Christopher or else be automatically refunded to Amanda.

In this case, Bill and Christopher function as "nodes" on the network. Nodes on the Lightning Network are in some ways analogous to miners on the Bitcoin network. They function as the servers that process the transactions on the network in a decentralized manner. Like miners, they do not have any control over the funds they help to move. Bill cannot steal Amanda's funds, as he will only receive the sender's incoming payment if he has already sent the outgoing payment to the recipient. Thus, receiving a payment is dependent on having already forwarded it. Lightning Network payments are conditional upon disclosure of a cryptographic secret, and knowledge of that secret allows for redemption from prior nodes (i.e. when Dan redeems from Christopher, Christopher can now redeem from Bill).

What happens, though, if Bill suddenly goes offline? Are the funds stuck forever in a 2-of-2 payment channel? To deal with unreliable nodes, the Lightning Network has built-in smart contract mechanisms such that users can unilaterally close any of their channels. It uses a "hashed time lock contract" to ensure that if Bill disappears, Amanda can always claw her money back. There is a time value set on this contract, usually in hours or days, so that Amanda can get repaid even if Bill's server is down.

Similarly, what happens if Amanda sends funds from her multi signature address to Dan on the Lightning Network but then tries to renege the payment? She could do this by falsely broadcasting an older transaction to the blockchain, thereby attempting to close out the channel in the state it was in before she sent the transaction to Dan. While Lightning software will delete these old transaction states, Amanda could potentially have changed the software to save it. If Amanda tries to claim she still has her old balance, Dan's software (or other designated servers) will monitor the blockchain for such a transaction, and when it catches Amanda's broadcasted transaction, she will lose all of her funds to Dan as a penalty. As a result, this creates a disincentive for anyone to try to broadcast an old, invalid ledger state.

What if Amanda and Bill are both online and willing to close their channel? If both parties co-operatively close a payment channel, the funds can be cleared to the blockchain in 10 minutes, or the current amount of time that it takes for a bitcoin transaction to confirm. Amanda and Bill may have transacted 'offline' thousands of times on the Lightning Network in the interim.

The Lightning Network ultimately relies on the underlying blockchain, be it Bitcoin's or otherwise, for its security. In the case of Bitcoin, it uses the underlying proof-of-work algorithm that secures the entire network to secure the Lightning Network as well. The blockchain is the ultimate arbiter, or in effect an automated judge. With the Lightning Network, you always know how the judge will decide, because it is pre-written into the transactions used to create the payment channels that make up the Lightning Network. This is a judge that cannot be cajoled, or bribed, or influenced. In effect, the Lightning Network allows for a "local consensus" state which is ultimately enforced by the "global consensus" (the blockchain). This local consensus state does not have custodial trust similar to traditional models, as any participant can unilaterally close out and redeem their funds without the cooperation other participants. Ultimately, the Lightning Network utilises the underlying blockchain as a means to batch settle transactions that have occurred off-chain without counterparty trust.

The Lightning Network can work on the Bitcoin blockchain, on other blockchains, or it can be used to instantly transfer different assets between blockchains using "cross-chain atomic swaps." (i.e. Bitcoin to Litecoin atomic swaps) The consensus rules for each blockchain can be different, allowing for secure crossing of asset classes without custodial clearing agencies.

With Lightning, small 'micro-transactions' or 'micro-payments' can flow through the network similar to how packets flow through the Internet. The technology has the potential to create new use cases that were not previously possible, such as machine-to-machine payments, content micropayments, and instant asset swaps.

Summary of The Lightning Networks Key Features

Instant Payments. Lightning-fast blockchain payments without worrying about block confirmation times. Security is enforced by blockchain smart-contracts without creating an on-blockchain transaction for individual payments. Payment speed measured in milliseconds to seconds.

Scalability. Capable of millions to billions of transactions per second across the network. Capacity blows away legacy payment rails by many orders of magnitude. Attaching payment per action/click is now possible without custodians.

Low Cost. By transacting and settling off-blockchain, the Lightning Network allows for exceptionally low fees, which allows for emerging use cases such as instant micropayments.

Cross Blockchains. Cross-chain atomic swaps can occur off-chain instantly with heterogeneous blockchain consensus rules. So long as the chains can support the same cryptographic hash function, it is possible to make transactions across blockchains without trust in 3rd party custodians.

Bitcoin Halving

Before going any deeper into the effects of bitcoin halving, let's cover some basic concepts relating to the bitcoin mining process. The creation of a new transaction prompts information to be sent to all the other nodes present on the bitcoin network, along with the ones making contributions to the overall mining process. The information from these transactions gets stored locally, and miners get rewarded for publishing this block of a transaction on to the blockchain ledger. In order to do this, miners have to contribute their computing power (hash rate) so as to solve a challenge requiring high processing power. The reward that a miner gets for successfully publishing a transaction depends on the block reward. Currently, the block reward is set at 12.5 BTC per block.

What is Bitcoin Halving?

In all the time that Bitcoin has been available on the market, it has followed a code that was written back in 2009 by the anonymous Satoshi Nakamoto. One of the many factors that have made Bitcoin so highly valuable is the limit on the total supply of Bitcoin – set at 21 million. This is hardcoded into the Bitcoin source code, causing Bitcoin to act under the same market influences as other limited resources such as gold. Bitcoin is considered the first 'deflationary' currency (as opposed to inflationary currencies such as the British Sterling or US Dollar, where there is no upper limit and more supply can be printed at will – lowering the purchasing power of a single unit).

Before heading on to the formal definition of bitcoin halving, let us consider two factors that affect the mining rewards. To make things somewhat competitive, the code of bitcoin was written in such a way so as to make miners compete against each other to obtain the reward. Hence, the greater the number of miners there are on a network, the higher the difficulty becomes for a single miner to obtain the reward. With an increase in the competition, miners tend to make use of greater processing power hence ruling out the likelihood of anyone making a profit through the use of a regular computers GPU. Nowadays, bitcoin mining requires the processing power of whole data centers.

What is the second factor? Well, this is where the definition of halving lies. According to the Bitcoin source code, **the reward of mining a block successfully gets cut in half after every 210000 blocks are mined.**

The event when the mining reward is cut in half is known as 'bitcoin halving'. This reward is always split into two equal halves. So for instance, if the Bitcoin reward of mining a block is currently set at 12.5 Bitcoins (2018 reward level), at the next halving event the reward level for each block successfully mined would be equal to 6.25 Bitcoins per block.

Are the halving events necessary?

A Bitcoin halving event pretty much simulates assets such as diamonds and gold that do not work in the same manner as fiat currency. Consider that the total amount of gold and diamonds in the world is essentially fixed. Hence, their value depends on how much of these commodities are currently available on the world market vs the current demand for the asset.

A halving event also works to preserve the value of the cryptocurrency, since it further limits the supply of newly mined Bitcoin entering the market. Assuming demand remains equal, according to the market rules of supply and demand, this reduced supply will push up the market value of the asset. At the same time, a halving event generally means that many miners with older setups might not make substantial profits anymore, as difficulty will remain constant despite the reduced payout. This would lead them towards shutting their equipment off. According to research from Lingham, the next halving event could lead to the shut off of approximately 25% of the mining rigs currently in operation as of 2017. In a case where the majority of miners shut off their equipment, the price of the Bitcoins would likely drop. However, given the current Bitcoin market cap this seems unlikely to happen.

As a reference point, the last halving event resulted in a drop of 20% of the bitcoin networks hashrate! However given the recent growth in Bitcoins value, and the difference in market conditions, we should be careful to draw too many conclusions from this data alone.

When is the next Bitcoin halving event?

Based on current mining rates, the estimated date for the next Bitcoin halving event is 31 May 2020. As previously noted, the current block reward for Bitcoin as of 2018 is set at 12.5 Bitcoin per block, with each block confirming roughly 2500 transactions in general. After the next halving event, this block reward will be halved to 6.25 Bitcoin per block.

As noted earlier, the price of Bitcoins is currently expected to rise following the next halving event. After the halving event there will be a lesser number of Bitcoins left to mine, meaning miners will be working with reduced profit margins in the short term and competing with each other like never before until the difficulty resets (if the network hash rate drops).

Even though bitcoin halving events will generally have a net negative impact on the mining communities, the representatives of the bitcoin mining community including Jihan Wu and Valery Vavilov are quite optimistic that as of now, there won't be a noticeable negative change on the bitcoin network other than a slight drop in the hashrate following the next halving event.

One interesting fact to note is that after the halving event, even though the bitcoin reward for each block would be cut in half, a miner may still receive a bigger value in terms of USD or GBP as compared to before the halving event. With the supply of newly mined Bitcoins now further limited, assuming constant demand the USD or GBP value of each Bitcoin will now increase. Depending on demand, this increase in the value of each coin may compensate the loss of coins in the block reward

References

[1] "Bitcoin: A Peer-to-Peer Electronic Cash System" - https://bitcoin.org/bitcoin.pdf

[2] "Capital Gains Tax: Annual Exempt Allowance For Tax Year 2018 to 2019" - https://www.gov.uk/government/publications/capital-gains-tax-annual-exempt-amount-for-tax-year-2018-to-2019/capital-gains-tax-annual-exempt-amount-for-tax-year-2018-to-2019

Acknowledgements

Thank you to my wife Christina for your patience, and for trusting my hunch back in 2014 to get invested into the Bitcoin space. Your continued trust and support is invaluable to my continued risk taking and entrepreneurial spirit.

Thank you to my friend Rob, who introduced me to an article about Bitcoin back in 2013. This article sparked a passion into this space that has accumulated more hours than I care to admit of research over the past 5 years.

Thank you to Satoshi Nakamoto, whoever you may be, for bringing this incredible technology into the world. Although I doubt even you could have predicted the path it has taken since you set it loose.

And finally, thank you to you – my readers. I hope you found this book interesting and informative. I wish you all the best in your discovery of Bitcoin. It's an exciting journey, remember to enjoy it.

About The Author:

29-year-old Charles Stephens is a former Software Engineer, entrepreneur, investor and author.

Charles first initially entered the world of Cryptocurrency in 2014 with an investment into Bitcoin after spending months researching the fledgling currency . Charles is now an expert in the Cryptocurrency space, having built an impressive Cryptocurrency portfolio and investments in several Ethereum ICO venture's.

Charles' latest venture is to share his knowledge and insight on the Cryptocurrency space, with the goal of breaking down seemingly complex and intimidating topics into simple and easy-to-read formats.

Printed in Great Britain
by Amazon

60264196R00028